CELEBRATING MARY

A COLLECTION

of

PRAISES AND PRAYERS

CELEBRATING MARY

A COLLECTION

of

PRAISES AND PRAYERS

Copyright © 2013 by The Word Among Us Press

Published by The Word Among Us Press
7115 Guilford Drive, Suite 100
Frederick, Maryland 21704
www.wau.org

17 16 15 14 13   1 2 3 4 5

ISBN: 978-1-59325-159-8
eISBN: 978-1-59325-452-0

Cover design by John Hamilton Designs

Cover image:
Carlo Maratta, (1625–1713) (studio of). *Virgin Reading
Surrounding by Angels.* Photo: Thierry Le Mage.
Location: Musee Magnin, Dijon, France
Photo Credit: © RMN-Grand Palais/Art Resource, NY

Interior images of Mary © Thinkstock Photos

Selections of papal quotations are used with permission of
Libreria Editrice Vaticana and can be found on the Vatican
website at www.vatican.va.

Poems "Visitation Day" and "Pietà," copyright © 2003 by
Jeanne Kun. "A Prayer for Refugges," copyright © 2007 by
Ken Gavin, SJ. "Prayer for My Daughter," copyright © 2007
by Suzanne Nussey. Used with permission. All rights reserved.
Selections from *Mary and the Christian Life* used with permission
of Amy Welborn. All rights reserved.

Made and printed in the United States of America

Library of Congress Control Number: 2013942864

Contents

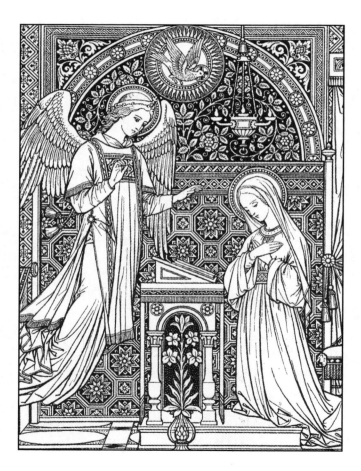

INTRODUCTION

When we praise her, love her, honor her, or give anything to her, it is God who is praised, God who is loved, God who is glorified.
~St. Louis de Montfort

Why has the Church since its beginnings given such praise and honor to Mary? She is, of course, the mother of our Lord. She carried Jesus in her womb, cared for him as a toddler and young boy, and stood by him at the foot of the cross. As the one who was closer to Jesus than any other human being that ever lived, we would naturally want to give Mary all honor and praise.

It's also true, as St. Louis de Montfort notes in one of the selections in this book, that when we praise and honor Mary, it is God who is praised and loved. We can't celebrate Mary without also celebrating God's love and mercy. Our Father loved us so much that he sent his Son into the world to save it. Mary said yes to God, and so the Word became flesh and dwelt among us.

Each of the one hundred "praises and prayers" in this book, gathered from both ancient and contemporary sources, highlights one aspect of the Blessed

Mother that deserves our reflection and gratitude. (For some of the older sources, we took the liberty of updating the archaic language.) As you pray through these selections, keep in mind that we are not just celebrating something that happened in the past. Mary was born two thousand years ago, in a very different time and culture, but as Mother of the Church, she continues to participate today in God's saving plan. She nurtures us, her sons and daughters, just as she did Jesus. What a blessing it is to know that Mary loves us and wants us to come ever closer to her son Jesus! We can have absolute confidence that she hears our prayers and continuously intercedes for us before the heavenly throne.

We pray that this little book will stir up your love and devotion to Mary, Mother of God, Mother of the Church, and Mother to each of us as well.

The Word Among Us Press

From St. Thérèse's Last Poem, "Why I Love You, O Mary!"

Oh! I would like to sing, Mary, why I love you,
Why your sweet name thrills my heart,
And why the thought of your supreme greatness
Could not bring fear to my soul.
If I gazed on you in your sublime glory,
Surpassing the splendor of all the blessed,
I could not believe that I am your child.
O Mary, before you I would lower my eyes! . . .

Soon I'll hear that sweet harmony.
Soon I'll go to beautiful Heaven to see you.
You who came to smile at me in the morning
of my life,
Come smile at me again . . . Mother . . .
It's evening now ! . . .
I no longer fear the splendor of your supreme glory.
With you I've suffered and now I want
To sing on your lap, Mary, why I love you,
And to go on saying that I am your child!

~ St. Thérèse of Lisieux

Mary, You Are . . .

You are, after God, O loving Mother,
the heavenly dew that alone tempers my suffering;
the light that dispels the darkness of my
understanding;
my guide in my pilgrimage here below;
my strength in my weakness;
my consolation in my tears;
my refuge in my danger.

~ St. Germanus of Constantinople

Mary, Teach Us Love

Mary, teach us love.
We ask you for love, Mary, love for Christ,
the only love, the highest love,
total love, giving love,
love in sacrifice for our brothers and sisters.
Help us to love in this way.

Obtain for us, O Mary, faith,
supernatural faith,
simple faith, full and strong,
sincere faith,
derived from its true source, the Word of God,
and from its flawless conduit,
the Magisterium,
established and guaranteed by Christ,
the living faith!

~Prayer of Pope Paul VI

4

Star of the Sea

Know, whoever you may be, that your life here below is but a voyage full of perils, in the midst of storms and tempests. Unless you wish to be shipwrecked, turn not your eyes from the star of the sea. When the tempests of temptation rage around you, look upon that star; call upon Mary.

If, overwhelmed with the enormity of your sins, covered with confusion at the hideous sores of your heart, terrified by the fear of punishment, you feel yourself enveloped in the darkness of sadness and gloom, and ready to sink into the abyss that yawns beneath your feet, look upon that star and invoke the name of Mary. In danger, anguish, and perplexity, call upon Mary; say, "Mary." Let that name never be far from your lips, far from your heart; but, that you may render yourself worthy to share the grace it brings with it, forget not the examples of which it will remind you.

~St. Bernard of Clairvaux

Nighttime Prayer to Mary

Mary, assist me in my needs.
Intercede for me with God in life and death.
Show your maternal kindness.
Present your children's prayers to God
who chose you for his Mother.

~Prayer said each night by
St. John Neumann in childhood

6

O Mother of Priests

O Mary,
Mother of Jesus Christ and Mother of priests,
accept this title which we bestow on you
to celebrate your motherhood
and to contemplate with you the priesthood
of your Son and of your sons,
O holy Mother of God.

O Mother of Christ,
to the Messiah-priest you gave a body of flesh
through the anointing of the Holy Spirit
for the salvation of the poor and the contrite of heart;
guard priests in your heart and in the Church,
O Mother of the Savior.

O Mother of Faith,
you accompanied to the Temple the Son of Man,
the fulfillment of the promises given to the fathers;
give to the Father for his glory
the priests of your Son,
O Ark of the Covenant.

O Mother of the Church,
in the midst of the disciples in the upper room,
you prayed to the Spirit
for the new people and their shepherds;
obtain for the Order of Presbyters
a full measure of gifts,
O Queen of the Apostles.

O Mother of Jesus Christ,
you were with him at the beginning
of his life and mission,
you sought the Master among the crowd,
you stood beside him
when he was lifted up from the earth,
consumed as the one eternal sacrifice,
and you had John, your son, near at hand;
accept from the beginning those who have been called,
protect their growth,
in their life ministry accompany your sons,
O Mother of Priests. Amen.

~Blessed John Paul II,
Apostolic Exhortation, *Pastores Dabo Vobis*

Mary: Giving Human Nature to God

That is what it meant to Mary to give
   human nature to God.
He was invulnerable; He asked her for a body
   to be wounded.
He was God; He asked her to make Him man.
He asked for hands and feet to be nailed.
He asked for flesh to be scourged.
He asked for blood to be shed.
He asked for a heart to be broken.
The stable at Bethlehem was the first Calvary.
The wooden manger was the first Cross.
The swaddling bands were the first burial bands.
The Passion had begun.
Christ was Man.

~Caryll Houselander, *The Reed of God*

From "Lines for a Drawing of Our Lady of the Night"

This, could I paint my inward sight,
This were Our Lady of the Night: . . .

The mantle which she holds on high
Is the great mantle of the sky.

Think, O sick toiler, when the night
Comes on thee, sad and infinite,

Think, sometimes 'tis our own Lady
Spreads her blue mantle over thee,

And holds the earth a wearied thing,
Beneath its gentle shadowing;

Then rest a little, and in sleep
Forget to weep, forget to weep!

~Francis Thompson

We Greet You, Mother of God

We greet you, Mother of God,
you venerable treasure of the whole world,
you inextinguishable lamp,
crown of virginity,
scepter of orthodox doctrine,
everlasting temple,
dwelling of him whom no dwelling can contain!
Mother and virgin, we greet you!
—you who in your virginal womb
enclosed the Measureless and Incomprehensible,
through whom the Holy Trinity was glorified
and adored.

~St. Cyril of Alexandria

A Message of Joy

In what words did the angel break the happy news of redemption? "Hail [rejoice], you that are full of grace, the Lord is with thee." The messenger of joy in his first word bid her to rejoice. He knew well that his message was one of good tidings of great joy to men, yes, to all creatures—a message of healing to all sicknesses. He knew well that his message was a message of God's light to a dark world. . . . He knew well that it told of salvation to all the fallen children of Adam, groaning under that yoke of the curse that fell on them when they were thrust out of Eden and banished from that happy home. . . .

It was fitting that God's proclamation of joy should open with the accents of gladness. And this is the reason why the angel named joy first, because he knew the coming fruits of his message, and that his exchange with the Virgin was to bring joy to the whole world.

~St. Sophronius of Jerusalem

From "The Akathist Hymn to the Theotokos"

The Archangel was sent from Heaven to cry "Rejoice!"
to the Theotokos. And beholding You, O Lord, taking
bodily form, he stood in awe, and with his bodiless
voice, he cried aloud to her such things as these:
Rejoice, you through whom joy shall shine forth.
Rejoice, you whom the curse will vanish.
Rejoice, the Restoration of fallen Adam.
Rejoice, the Redemption of the tears of Eve.
Rejoice, O Height beyond human logic.
Rejoice, O Depth invisible even to the eyes of angels.
Rejoice, for you are the King's throne.
Rejoice, you bear Him, Who bears the universe.
Rejoice, O Star revealing the Sun.
Rejoice, O Womb of divine Incarnation.
Rejoice, you through whom creation is renewed.
Rejoice, you through whom the Creator is born a Babe.
Rejoice, O Bride Ever-Virgin.

~Traditional Eastern Orthodox Hymn

12

Mary: The Shortest Way to Jesus

Mary can help us to love Jesus best; she is the one who can show us the shortest way to Jesus. Mary was the one whose intercession led Jesus to work the first miracle. "They have no wine," she said to Jesus. "Do whatever he tells you," she said to the servants. We take the part of the servants. Let us go to her with great love and trust. We are serving Jesus in the distressing disguise of the poor.

~Blessed Mother Teresa of Calcutta

Grace Makes Us Like God

When the angel saluted Our Lady, he did not call her "Mary"; he called her "full of grace," as if those words expressed her better than a name. . . . And indeed, one may say that when we think of her, grace seems precisely the word that expresses her.

In this world, there is nothing so precious and nothing so beautiful as grace. To understand this, we need only remember that in heaven it will be changed into glory. Grace makes us like God. Without it we are dead; with it we live the life of God and are made partakers of his nature. If we could see a soul clothed in divine grace, we should see a sight to which no beauty on earth could compare. . . . One degree of grace, if it could be put before us in a tangible form, would outweigh and outshine the costliest jewel.

~Mother Francis Raphael, OSD

In Your Faithful Care

Most Holy Mary, my mother and advocate,
to your faithful care and special keeping
and to the bosom of your mercy,
today and every day,
and particularly at the hour of my death,
I commend my soul and my body.
All my hope and consolation,
all my trials and miseries,
my life and the end of my life,
I commit to you,
that through your most holy intercession
and by your merits,
all my works and actions
may be directed and ordered
according to your will
and that of your divine Son.

~St. Aloysius Gonzaga

Mary, Most Blessed

The God, whom earth and sea and sky
adore and laud and magnify,
whose might they own, whose praise they tell,
in Mary's body deigned to dwell.

O Mother blest! The chosen shrine,
wherein the Architect divine,
whose hand contains the earth and sky,
vouchsafed in hidden guise to lie.

Blest in the message Gabriel brought;
blest in the work the Spirit wrought;
most blest, to bring to human birth
the long desired of all the earth.

~Venantius Fortunatus

Mary Shares Christ's Pain . . . and Ours

I saw a part of the compassion of our Lady, St. Mary: for Christ and she were so "oned" in love that the greatness of her loving was cause of the greatness of her pain. For in this I saw a substance of nature's love, continued by grace, that creatures have toward him, which kind love was most fully and exceedingly shown in his sweet mother. For so much as she loved him more than all other, her pains exceeded all other; for the higher, the mightier, the sweeter the love be, the more sorrow it is to the lover to see that body in pain that is loved. . . .

Here I saw a great "oneing" between Christ and us, to my understanding: for when he was in pain, we were in pain. And all creatures that might suffer pain suffered with him.

~Blessed Julian of Norwich

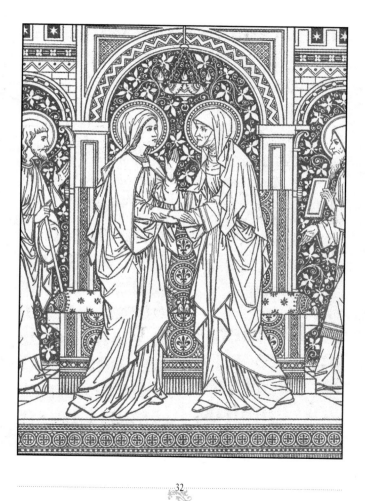

Visitation Day

In haste Mary climbed the hills of Judah,
a young girl
hurried by the secret growing in her
to seek reassurance
from another who
also held in quiet confidence
the certainty that nothing is impossible with God.

And Elizabeth did not fail her:
Blessed are you among women,
and blessed is the fruit of your womb.
The Spirit prompted her
to instant recognition
of Mary's hidden treasure
as her own babe leapt within her womb,
already eager to commence his herald role.

Then Mary spilled her joy
(forever scattering grace about her)

in words that long millennia
have never silenced.

And all generations since that Visitation Day
have called her blessed
as they too magnify the Word
so wondrously clothed in this virgin's flesh.

~Jeanne Kun

Under Thy Protection

Under thy protection
we seek refuge,
Holy Mother of God;
despise not our petitions
in our needs,
but from all dangers
deliver us always,
Virgin Glorious and Blessed.

~*Sub Tuum Praesidium,* ancient hymn

Let My Future Radiant Shine

At morn, at noon, at twilight dim,
Maria, thou hast heard my hymn:
In joy and woe, in good and ill,
Mother of God, be with me still.
When the hours flew brightly by,
And not a cloud obscured the sky,
My soul, lest it should truant be,
Thy grace did guide to thine and thee.
Now, when storms of fate o'ercast
Darkly my present and my past,
Let my future radiant shine
With sweet hopes of thee and thine.

~Edgar Allan Poe

Show Us Jesus

Holy Mary, Mother of God,
you have given the world its true light,
Jesus, your Son—the Son of God.
You abandoned yourself completely
to God's call
and thus became a wellspring
of the goodness which flows forth from him.
Show us Jesus. Lead us to him.
Teach us to know and love him,
so that we too can become
capable of true love
and be fountains of living water
in the midst of a thirsting world.

~Pope Benedict XVI, Encyclical Letter,
Deus Caritas Est

More Mother Than Queen

Oh, how I love our blessed Lady! Had I been a priest, how I would have sung her praises! She is spoken of as unapproachable, whereas she should be represented as easy of imitation. . . . She is more mother than queen. I have heard it said that her splendor eclipses that of all the saints as the rising sun makes all the stars disappear. It sounds so strange. That a mother should take away the glory of her children! I think quite the reserve. I believe that she will greatly increase the splendor of the elect.

~St. Thérèse of Lisieux

God Let Himself Be Carried

God-made-man has found his liberty in seeing himself imprisoned in [Mary's] womb. He had made his omnipotence shine forth in letting himself be carried by that blessed virgin. He has found his glory and his Father's in hiding his splendors from all creatures here below, and revealing them to Mary only. He has glorified his independence and his majesty in depending on that sweet virgin, in his conception, in his birth, in his presentation in the Temple, in his hidden life of thirty years, and even in his death, where she was to be present, in order that he might make with her but one same sacrifice and be immolated to the eternal Father by her consent, just as Isaac of old was offered by Abraham's consent to the will of God. It is she who has suckled him, nourished him, supported him, brought him up, and then sacrificed him for us.

~St. Louis de Montfort

The Ideal for Every Woman

As Mother of God and mother of all God's children, Mary is exalted above all creatures on the throne of glory; maternity itself is glorified through her. As Virgin, she manifests an incomparable beauty pleasing to God, along with the fruitfulness of virginal purity. As Queen, she evidences the conquering power of a serving love and of purity intact. Every woman who wants to fulfill her destiny must look to Mary as the ideal.

~St. Teresa Benedicta of the Cross
(Edith Stein)

A Clear and Shining Light

You, O Virgin, are like a clear and shining sky in which God has set his tent. From you he comes forth like a bridegroom leaving his chamber. Like a giant running his course, he will run the course of his life, which will bring salvation for all who will ever live, and extending from the highest heavens to the end of them, it will fill all things with divine warmth and with life-giving brightness.

~St. Sophronius of Jerusalem

Come to Our Aid

Come to our aid, O most compassionate Mother, without regarding our many sins. Remember again and again that our Creator has taken human flesh from you, not to condemn sinners, but to save them. If you had been made Mother of God only for your own advantage, it might be said that it would hardly matter to you whether we were saved or condemned. But God has clothed himself with your flesh for your salvation and for that of all. What use to us is your power and glory, if you do not allow us to share your joy? Aid us and protect us. Remember that we need your assistance. We recommend ourselves to you; save us and make us serve and eternally love your Son Jesus Christ.

~St. Anselm

Mary, Sorrowful Mother

Mary, sorrowful Mother,
you are a silent witness of these decisive moments
for the history of salvation.
Give us your eyes so that on the face of the
Crucified One, disfigured by pain,
we may recognize the image of the glorious Risen One.
Help us to embrace him and entrust ourselves to him,
so that we be made worthy of his promises.
Help us to be faithful today and throughout our lives.
Amen!

~Blessed John Paul II,
World Youth Day, April 13, 2003

Ave Maria Stellis

Hail, bright star of ocean,
God's own Mother blest,
Ever sinless Virgin,
Gate of heavenly rest.

Taking that sweet Ave,
Which from Gabriel came,
Peace confirm within us,
Changing Eva's name.

Break the captives' fetters,
Light on blindness pour,
All our ills expelling,
Every bliss implore.

Show thyself a Mother;
May the Word Divine,
Born for us thy Infant,
Hear our prayers through thine.

Virgin all excelling,
Mildest of the mild,
Freed from guilt, preserve us,
Pure and undefiled.

Keep our life all spotless,
Make our way secure,
Till we find in Jesus,
Joy forevermore.

Through the highest heaven
To the Almighty Three,
Father, Son, and Spirit,
One same glory be. Amen.

~Traditional

Mary, Help Me to Fulfill My Earthly Vocation

O Mary, help me to keep to my purpose of living as a faithful disciple of Jesus, for the building up of the Christian society and the joy of the holy Catholic Church. I greet you, Mother, morning and evening; I pray to you as I go on my way; from you I hope for the inspiration and encouragement that will enable me to fulfill the sacred promises of my earthly vocation, give glory to God, and win eternal salvation. O Mary! Like you in Bethlehem and on Golgotha, I too wish to stay always close to Jesus. He is the eternal King of all ages and all peoples. Amen.

~Blessed John XXIII

Shelter Us

Mother of almighty God!
Suppliant at thy feet we pray;
Shelter us from Satan's fraud,
Safe beneath the wing this day.

~Anonymous, eighteenth century

A Prayer for Refugees

Mary, strong and true, as a young mother you knew the fear of flight and felt its wrenching grip. Accompany refugees exiled from their homes; tenderly lead them to a safe place. Teach us to be enduring friends to families forced to move.

Mary, compassionate mother, watch over migrant children wandering in foreign lands. Guide them as they search for family and a future. Be their steady and sure road toward home.

Mary, lady of sorrows, in pain and confusion you watched your child suffer. Comfort displaced women battered by raw cruelty. Be a light for their journey, a shelter and warm embrace.

Mary, loving mother, in Jesus you found nourishment for the world's hungers. Let us taste and feel the hunger of refugees in distress. With the love of the risen Christ, may we fill their needs.

~Ken Gavin, SJ

Mother, Teach Us How to Say Yes

We can turn to [Mary] in grave humility and say to her, "Look, you are one of us. Teach us the height to which we can rise. We can't bear Christ, but we can be pregnant with love for every human being, men and women alike, in giving life to other people. Mother, teach us how to do it. Teach us how to love. Teach us how to hope. Teach us how to say 'yes' to the impossible."

~Catherine de Hueck Doherty

Prayer to Our Lady of Guadalupe

Our Lady of Guadalupe,
Mystical Rose,
make intercession for holy Church,
protect the sovereign pontiff,
help all those who invoke you in their necessities,
and since you are the ever Virgin Mary
and Mother of the true God,
obtain for us from your most holy Son
the grace of keeping our faith,
of sweet hope in the midst of the bitterness of life,
of burning charity, and the precious gift
of final perseverance.
Amen.

~Traditional

Salutation of the Blessed Virgin

Hail, O Lady, Holy Queen,
Mary, holy Mother of God:
you are the Virgin made Church
chosen by the Most Holy Father in heaven.
whom he consecrated with His most holy beloved Son
and with the Holy Spirit the Paraclete,
in whom there was and is all fullness of
grace and every good.

Hail His Palace! Hail His Tabernacle!
Hail His Dwelling! Hail His Robe!
Hail His Servant! Hail His Mother!

And hail all You holy virtues
which are poured into the hearts of the faithful
through the grace and enlightenment
of the Holy Spirit,
that from being unbelievers,
you may make them faithful to God.

~St. Francis of Assisi

From "Herself a Rose Who Bore the Rose"

Herself a rose, who bore the Rose,
She bore the Rose and felt its thorn.
All loveliness newborn
Took on her bosom its repose,
And slept and woke there night and morn.

Lily herself, she bore the one
Fair Lily; sweeter, whiter, far
Than she or others are:
The Sun of Righteousness her Son,
She was his morning star. . . .

Christ's mirror she of grace and love,
Of beauty and of life and death:
By hope and love and faith
Transfigured to his likeness, "Dove,
Spouse, Sister, Mother," Jesus saith.

~Christina Rossetti

The Highest Mountain

It was surely of the Most Blessed Virgin that Isaiah spoke (2:2) when he said that there should be a mountain of the house of the Lord, whose foundations would be on the top of the holy mountains, for by the dignity of her election and the sanctity of her life, she surpassed all others most beloved and favored by God. To have the exalted privilege of conceiving the eternal Word, the greatness of her merits should reach far above all the choirs of angels, to the very throne of the Divinity.

~St. Gregory the Great

Prayer of Total Consecration

O Immaculata, Queen of Heaven and Earth, refuge of sinner and most loving Mother, God has willed to entrust the entire order of mercy on to you. I, (name), a repentant sinner, cast myself at your feet, humbly imploring you to take me with all that I am and have, wholly to yourself as your possession and property. Please make of me, of all my powers of soul and body, of my whole life, death and eternity, whatever most pleases you. If it pleases you, use all that I am and have without reserve, wholly to accomplish what was said of you: "She will crush your head" and "You alone have destroyed all the heresies in the world."

Let me be a fit instrument in your immaculate and merciful hands for introducing and increasing your glory to the maximum in all the many strayed and indifferent souls, and thus help extend as far as possible the blessed kingdom of the most Sacred Heart of Jesus. For wherever you enter, you obtain the grace of conversion and growth in holiness, since it is through your hands that all graces come to us from the most Sacred Heart of Jesus.

~St. Maximilian Kolbe

I Am Certain of Your Help

Do not tell me, O Gracious Virgin, that you cannot grant my request, for your beloved Son has given you all power in heaven and on earth. Do not tell me that you ought not, for you are the common mother of all the poor children of Adam, and particularly of me. I am then certain that you will lend me your help and assistance.

~St. Francis de Sales

Fly to This Mother

It was not a woman of wealth and grandeur that the Son of the living God chose for his mother, but a lowly virgin whose soul was adorned with every virtue. For as the Blessed Virgin Mary had preserved her virginity in the most stainless and pure condition, she was made worthy to conceive, in her chaste womb, Christ our Lord. To this most holy virgin and Mother of God, then, let us have recourse and become participators in the fruits of her powerful intercession.

Oh, all you who seek to preserve holy purity, fly to this tender and chaste mother of our Lord and Master.

~St. John Chrysostom

The Son Values Her Prayers

When this Mother, whom the saints call an altar of mercy upon which sinners are reconciled to God, asks grace of Jesus for us, the Son values her prayers so highly and desires so ardently to gladden her heart that she seems to command rather than petition, and appears to us more like a queen than a handmaid.

~St. Peter Damian

My Soul Magnifies the Lord

May Mary's soul be in each one to magnify the Lord;
may Mary's spirit be in each one to rejoice in God. If,
according to the flesh, the Mother of Christ is one alone,
according to the faith, all souls bring forth Christ; each,
in fact, welcomes the Word of God within. . . .

Mary's soul magnifies the Lord and her spirit rejoices
in God because, consecrated in soul and spirit to the
Father and to the Son, she adores with devout affection
one God, from whom come all things, and only one Lord,
by virtue of whom all things exist.

~St. Ambrose

At the Cross with Mary

We don't know what went through Mary's mind as she watched her Son suffer and die. We can guess, and writers through history have used their imaginations to describe what she might have been feeling. A minor but intriguing theme of some medieval spiritual writing was that as she watched Jesus die, Mary experienced the birth pangs she had been spared thirty-three years before. But it's hard to say what she felt beyond the normal pain of a mother watching her son unjustly executed and the extraordinary pain of a sword through her heart as she went over and over the angel's promises so long ago.

Jesus said that whenever we encounter suffering, we encounter him (see Matthew 25:31-46). So it stands to reason that when we are present with suffering, we are present at the cross with Mary at our side. We watch her and we learn how to be present, which means how to love, simply and deeply.

~Amy Welborn,
Mary and the Christian Life

42

The Perfect Model

There are countless saints who have modeled for us how to follow Jesus, how to be conformed to him. From Francis, I learn Jesus' poverty; from Ignatius, Jesus' obedience; from the great Teresa of Avila, Jesus' prayer; from Thérèse of Lisieux, Jesus' simplicity; from Augustine, Jesus' wisdom; from Thomas Aquinas, Jesus' love of the truth; from the martyrs, Jesus' fidelity to death.

All these are models, yet imperfect models. The perfect model? The one fashioned by the Holy Spirit to embody the perfect response to Jesus? MARY. But even before Jesus was the model for her or anyone else, she was the model for him. How so? She was the mold from which the Holy Spirit fashioned God in the flesh—God from the flesh of Mary! Jesus' physical traits must have resembled hers. But more important, God chose her and made her to be the mold, the model if you will, for his humanity. Her flesh was sinless, made so by the one to be born of her. And so the humanity of Jesus was sinless, not merely because he was God, but because he took sinless flesh from Mary. A metallurgist knows that any imperfection in the mold for a gold medal will show up in the finished product. The mold for Jesus was perfect. And so was the product, Jesus' perfectly holy humanity.

~George Montague, SM,
Mary's Life in the Spirit

From "A Hymn before Battle"

Ah, Mary, pierced with sorrow,
Remember, reach and save
The soul that goes tomorrow
Before the God that gave!
Since each was born of woman,
For each, in utter need—
True comrade and brave foeman—
Madonna, intercede!

~Rudyard Kipling

Mother of God, Mother of the Redeemer

The Virgin Mary, who at the message of the angel received the Word of God in her heart and in her body and gave Life to the world, is acknowledged and honored as being truly the Mother of God and Mother of the Redeemer. Redeemed by reason of the merits of her Son and united to Him by a close and indissoluble tie, she is endowed with the high office and dignity of being the Mother of the Son of God, by which account she is also the beloved daughter of the Father and the temple of the Holy Spirit.

Because of this gift of sublime grace, she far surpasses all creatures, both in heaven and on earth. At the same time, however, because she belongs to the offspring of Adam she is one with all those who are to be saved. . . . Wherefore she is hailed as a preeminent and singular member of the Church, and as its type and excellent exemplar in faith and charity. The Catholic Church, taught by the Holy Spirit, honors her with filial affection and piety as a most beloved mother.

Second Vatican Council, *Lumen Gentium*

An Influx of Peace

While I was in the presence of the Blessed Sacrament, the Spirit of God caused me to speak with this divine mother. In an instant I felt that my prayer was heard and that something like a tangible garment was removed from me, that the entire sensitive part of my soul received an influx of peace. My aversion was changed into a cordial love for all those persons toward whom I experienced feelings of aversion and bitterness. When occasions presented themselves, I rendered these individuals all possible services, according to my state and condition. They couldn't understand this, for none except those to whom I rendered an account of my soul knew what was transpiring within me or the motives which caused me to conduct myself exteriorly in this way.

~Blessed Marie of the Incarnation

Hail, O Chaste One

Hail, O Chaste One,
who have crushed the serpent's head,
hurling him into the abyss.
Hail, O Refuge of the afflicted,
hail, Ransom of the curse.
Hail, O Mother of Christ,
Son of the Living God,
to whom shall be glory, honor,
adoration, and praise.

~St. Ephrem of Syria

The Fire of Holy Love

God who is charity appeared on earth in order to enkindle in all the fire of his holy love. But he inflamed no heart with his love so intensely as the heart of his mother, Mary, for being entirely free from all attachment to earthly things, she was most susceptible to this holy love.

~St. Alphonsus Liguori

The Echo of God

You never think of Mary without Mary, in your place, thinking of God. You never praise or honor Mary without Mary praising and honoring God. Mary is altogether relative to God; and, indeed, I might well call her the relation to God. She only exists with reference to God. She is the echo of God, who says nothing, repeats nothing, but God. If you say, "Mary," she says, "God."

St. Elizabeth praised Mary and called her blessed, because she had believed. Mary, the faithful echo of God, at once intoned, "My soul doth magnify the Lord." That which Mary did then she does daily now. When we praise her, love her, honor her, or give anything to her, it is God who is praised, God who is loved, God who is glorified. We give, then, to God by Mary and in Mary.

~St. Louis de Montfort

Mary Contemplates the Face of Christ

The contemplation of Christ has an incomparable model in Mary. In a unique way, the face of the Son belongs to Mary. It was in her womb that Christ was formed, receiving from her a human resemblance which points to an even greater spiritual closeness. No one has ever devoted himself to the contemplation of the face of Christ as faithfully as Mary. The eyes of her heart already turned to him at the Annunciation, when she conceived him by the power of the Holy Spirit. In the months that followed, she began to sense his presence and to picture his features. When at last she gave birth to him in Bethlehem, her eyes were able to gaze tenderly on the face of her Son, as she "wrapped him in swaddling cloths, and laid him in a manger" (Luke 2:7). Thereafter, Mary's gaze, ever filled with adoration and wonder, would never leave him.

~Blessed John Paul II, Apostolic Letter,
Rosarium Virginis Mariae

Our Last Hail Mary on Earth

How shall [our] last Hail Mary be said? Will death give us full warning, and shall we be aware that we are very near the end? Or shall we be taken suddenly away? Or shall death be preceded by a long or short interval of helplessness and unconsciousness, so that we shall for all spiritual purposes be dead long before the actual moment of death? Is any dying one ever so conscious that the end has come for him that he is able to change the familiar words, and adapt them to the actual circumstances? "Holy Mary, Mother of God, pray for me, a poor sinner, now, this moment; for this is indeed the hour of my death—and this is my last Hail Mary on earth, to be followed soon, I hope, by my first Hail Mary in heaven."

~Matthew Russell, SJ

Turning the World to God

Look carefully at Mary's prayer. For what is she praising God? Satisfying her needs, making her personally
"happy," or fixing her problems?

Not really. It seems as if she is praising and thank-
ing God for his power and his mercy and that she, his
handmaid, is playing a role in his plan of redemption,
of shaking the world out of its self-satisfaction and
self-reliance, turning that world radically, like the poor,
back to dependence on God.

~Amy Welborn, *Mary and the Christian Life*

Our Lady Who Goes in Haste

Our Lady, as soon as she had heard the news that she was to be the mother of Jesus and the announcement that her cousin Elizabeth was expecting a child—the Gospel says—she went to her in haste; she did not wait. She did not say, "But now I am with child; I must take care of my health; my cousin is bound to have friends who can care for her." Something stirred her and she "went with haste" to Elizabeth (cf. Luke 1:39). It is beautiful to think this of Our Lady, of our Mother, that she hastens, because she intends to help. She goes to help; she doesn't go to boast and tell her cousin, "Listen, I'm in charge now, because I am the Mother of God!" No, she did not do that. She went to help! And Our Lady is always like this. She is our Mother who always hurries to us whenever we are in need.

It would be beautiful to add to the Litany of Our Lady something like this: "O Lady who goes in haste, pray for us!" It is lovely, isn't? For she always goes in haste; she does not forget her children. And when her children are in difficulty, when they need something and call on her, she hurries to them. This gives us a security, the security of always having our Mother next to us, beside us. We move forward, we journey more easily in life when our mother is near. Let us think of this grace of Our Lady, this grace that she gives us: of being close to us, but without making us wait for her. Always! She—let us trust in this—she lives to help us, Our Lady who always hastens, for our sake.

~Pope Francis, Homily, May 26, 2013

From "The Grandeurs of Mary"

Inexhaustible wonder; the treasures of God
seem to multiply under thy marvelous hand;
And the power of thy Son seems to gain and to grow,
when he deigns to obey thy maternal command.

Ten thousand magnificent greatnesses blend
their vast oceans of light at the foot of thy throne;
Ten thousand unspeakable majesties grace
the royalty vested in Mary alone.

But look, what a wonder there is up in God!
One love, like a special perfection, we see;
And the chief of thy grandeurs, great Mother, is there—
in the love the Eternal himself has for thee.

~Frederick W. Faber

Memorare

Remember, O most gracious Virgin Mary,
 that never was it known that anyone
who fled to your protection,
implored your help,
or sought your intercession,
was left unaided.
Inspired with this confidence,
I fly to you, O Virgin of virgins, my Mother.
To you I come, before you I stand, sinful and sorrowful.
O Mother of the Word Incarnate,
despise not my petitions,
but in your mercy, hear and answer me.
Amen.

~Traditional

The Angelus

V. The Angel of the Lord declared unto Mary.
R. And she conceived of the Holy Spirit.
Hail Mary, full of grace,
The Lord is with thee;
Blessed art thou among women,
And blessed is the fruit of thy womb, Jesus.
Holy Mary, Mother of God,
Pray for us sinners,
Now and at the hour of our death. Amen.
V. Behold the handmaid of the Lord.
R. Be it done unto me according to thy word.
Hail Mary . . .
V. And the Word was made flesh.
R. And dwelt among us.
Hail Mary . . .

V. Pray for us, O Holy Mother of God.
R. That we may be made worthy of
the promises of Christ.

Let us pray: Pour forth, we beseech thee, O Lord, thy grace into our hearts, that we to whom the Incarnation of Christ thy Son was made known by the message of an angel, may by his passion and cross be brought to the glory of his resurrection. Through the same Christ Our Lord. Amen.

~Traditional

From "The Blessed Virgin Compared to the Air We Breathe"

I say that we are wound
With mercy round and round
As if with air: the same
is Mary, more by name.
She, wild web, wondrous robe,
Mantles the guilty globe,
Since God has let dispense
Her prayers his providence:
Nay, more than almoner,
The sweet alms' self is her,
And men are meant to share
Aer life as life does air. . . .

Be thou then, O thou dear
Mother, my atmosphere;

My happier world, wherein
To wend and meet no sin;
Above me, round me lie
Fronting my froward eye
With sweet and scarless sky;
Stir in my ears, speak there
Of God's love, O live air,
of patience, penance, prayer.
World-mothering air, air wild,
Wound with thee, in thee isled,
Fold home, fast fold thy child.

~Gerard Manley Hopkins, SJ

Come and Meet My Soul

Blessed is the man who loves your name, O Mary.
Yes, truly blessed is he who loves your sweet name,
O Mother of God!
Your name is so glorious and admirable,
that no one who remembers it
has any fears at the hour of death.
I ask you, O Mary,
for the glory of your name,
to come and meet my soul
when it is departing from this world,
and to take it in your arms.
Amen.

~St. Bonaventure

58

Like a Precious Oil

The name of Mary enlightens the mind, rejoices the heart, inspires the love of virtue and the courage to make a sacrifice. It cannot be pronounced without bringing some good to the soul. It is to the soul like a precious oil, healing its wounds, gratifying it by its delicious odor, and keeping alive in it the fire of divine love.

~St. Alphonsus Liguori

Mary's Words to St. Bridget

I am the Queen of Heaven. You were concerned about how you should give me praise. Know for certain that all praise of my Son is praise of me. And those who dishonor him dishonor me, since my love for him and his for me was so ardent that the two of us were like one heart. So highly did he honor me, who was an earthen vessel, that he raised me up above all the angels. Therefore, you should praise me like this:

Blessed are you, God, Creator of all things, who deigned to descend into the womb of the Virgin Mary.

Blessed are you, God, who willed to be in the Virgin Mary without being a burden to her and deigned to receive immaculate flesh from her without sin.

Blessed are you, God, who came to the Virgin, giving joy to her soul and to her whole body, and who went out of her to the sinless joy of her whole body.

Blessed are you, God, who after your ascension gladdened the Virgin Mary your Mother with frequent consolations and visited her with your consolation.

Blessed are you, God, who assumed the body and soul of the Virgin Mary, your Mother, into heaven and honored her by placing her next to your divinity above all the angels. Have mercy on me because of her prayers!

~St. Bridget of Sweden

60

Prayer for My Daughter

Mary, Mother of our Lord, my mother, the child I dreamed of all my life has arrived. Even as I hold her closely in my arms, I know a time will come when I must let her go. Good Mother, as you lovingly prepared your son Jesus to live in a world that did not love him, so help me, I pray, to nourish, love, and teach my child. Give me the ears to hear and the eyes to see the gift that is my daughter. Let me never shame her; grant me the patience and discernment to always give my blessing to the person God created her to be. May she grow strong in wisdom and in grace, able to stand firm in the assurance that she is beloved of God and of our family and so, with courage and compassion, serve your Son and the world that desperately needs his love. When the last day comes for me to hold her in my arms, help me to let go graciously in the knowledge that both of us, mother and child, are children of the kingdom and eternally yours.

~Suzanne Nussey

61

Beyond All Other Creature

Thou Virgin Mother, daughter of thy Son,
Humble and high beyond all other creature,
The limit fixed of the eternal counsel.
Thou art the one who such nobility
To human nature gave, that its Creator
Did not disdain to make himself its creature. . .

In thee compassion is, in thee is pity,
In thee magnificence; in thee unites
Whate'er of goodness is in any creature.

~Dante, from *The Divine Comedy*

62

Mary, Speak to Us of Jesus

Mary, Mother of the "Yes," you listened to Jesus,
and know the tone of his voice and
the beating of his heart.
Morning Star, speak to us of him,
and tell us about your journey of following him
on the path of faith.

Mary, who dwelt with Jesus in Nazareth,
impress on our lives your sentiments,
your docility, your attentive silence,
and make the Word flourish in genuinely free choices.

Mary, speak to us of Jesus, so that the freshness
of our faith
shines in our eyes and warms the heart of
those we meet,
as you did when visiting Elizabeth,
who in her old age rejoiced with you for the gift of life.

Mary, Virgin of the Magnificat,
help us to bring joy to the world and, as at Cana,
lead every young person involved in service of others
to do only what Jesus will tell them. . . .

Mary, Our Lady of Loreto, Gate of Heaven,
help us to lift our eyes on high.
We want to see Jesus, to speak with him,
to proclaim his love to all.

~Pope Benedict XVI, Prayer at the Shrine of Loreto and
Holy House, September 1, 2007

63

She Gave Hospitality to God

To others grace has been given in part, but to Mary the fullness of grace was given in its entirety. O Virgin, truly blessed, who has shown herself greater than the universe, for she contained within her him whom the universe could not contain; she carried him who upholds the world; she nourished him who gives food to all living creatures; she gave hospitality to God; and she obtains from him, in return, peace for earth and glory for heaven.

~St. Peter Chrysologus

64

Mary Sanctifies the Ordinary

We can't forget that Mary spent nearly every day of her life just like millions of other women who look after their families, bringing up their children and taking care of the house. Mary sanctifies the ordinary, everyday things—what some people wrongly regard as unimportant and insignificant: everyday work, looking after those closest to you, visits to friends and relatives. What a blessed ordinariness, that can be so full of love of God!

~St. Josemaría Escrivá

Guide Us Home

In you, O Mary, is fulfilled, as we can bear it, an original purpose of the Most High. He once had meant to come on earth in heavenly glory, but we sinned; and then he could not safely visit us, except with a shrouded radiance and a bedimmed majesty, for he was God. So he came himself in weakness, not in power; and he sent you, a creature, in his stead, with a creature's comeliness and luster suited to our state.

And now your very face and form, dear Mother, speak to us of the Eternal; not like earthly beauty, dangerous to look upon, but like the morning star, which is your emblem, bright and musical, breathing purity, telling of heaven, and infusing peace. O harbinger of day! O hope of the pilgrim! Lead us still as you have led; in the dark night, across the bleak wilderness, guide us on to our Lord Jesus; guide us home.

~Blessed John Henry Newman

Walk in Her Footsteps

In dangers, in doubts, in difficulties, think of Mary, call upon Mary. Let not her name depart from your lips, never suffer it to leave your heart. And that you may obtain the assistance of her prayer, neglect not to walk in her footsteps. With her for a guide, you shall never go astray; while invoking her, you shall never lose heart; so long as she is in your mind, you are safe from deception; while she holds your hand, you cannot fall; under her protection, you have nothing to fear; if she walks before you, you shall not grow weary; if she shows you favor, you shall reach the goal.

~St. Bernard of Clairvaux

67

Loveliest Mother

O loveliest and most loving Mother, hail!
You have given forth into this world your Son,
sent from heaven and breathed into you
by the Spirit of God.
Praised be the Father, the Son, and the Holy Spirit.
Breathed into you by the Holy Spirit.

~St. Hildegard of Bingen

Salve Regina (Hail, Holy Queen)

Hail, holy Queen, Mother of Mercy,
our life, our sweetness, and our hope.
To thee do we cry, poor banished children of Eve;
to thee do we send up our sighs,
mourning, and weeping in this valley of tears.

Turn then, most gracious advocate,
thine eyes of mercy toward us;
and after this our exile,
show unto us the blessed fruit of thy womb, Jesus.
O clement, O loving, O sweet Virgin Mary.

~Traditional

69

We Are Your Children

Holy Immaculate Mary, help all who are in trouble. Give courage to the fainthearted, console the sad, heal the infirm, pray for the people, intercede for the clergy, have a special care for nuns. May all feel, all enjoy your kind and powerful assistance, all who now and always render and will render you honor, and will offer you their petitions. Hear all our prayers, O Mother, and grant them all. We are all your children: Grant the prayers of your children. Amen forever.

~Blessed John XXIII

Mary as Mother Wisdom

I am the mother of fair love,
and of fear,
and of knowledge,
and of holy hope.
In me is all grace of the way and of truth,
in me is all hope of life, and of virtue.
Come over to me,
all ye that desire me,
and be filled with my fruits.
For my spirit is sweet above honey,
and my inheritance above honey and the honeycomb.
My memory is unto everlasting generations.

~Ecclesiasticus 24:24-28
(Douay Rheims translation)

As Long As I Need It

Mary, let love for you always be with me, and the care for me be always with you. Let the cry of my need, as long as it persists, be with you, and the care of your goodness, as long as I need it, be with me. Let joy in your blessedness be always with me, and compassion for my wretchedness, where I need it, be with you.

~St. Anselm

72

We Find Our Help

My sisters, you see how we find in Mary
everything we need.
We want grace; she is the "mother of divine grace."
We stand in need of wisdom; she is the "seat of wisdom."
We need an asylum against the chastisements of divine
justice; she is the "refuge of sinners."
We require assistance, and she is the "help of Christians."

~St. Jane Frances de Chantal

Bearing Christ in the World

Our Lady said yes for the human race. Each one of us must echo that yes for our own lives.

We are all asked if we will surrender what we are, our humanity, our flesh and blood, to the Holy Spirit and allow Christ to fill the emptiness formed by the particular shape in our life.

The surrender that is asked of us includes complete and absolute trust; it must be like Our Lady's surrender, without condition and without reservation.

We shall not be asked to do more than the Mother of God; we shall not be asked to become extraordinary or set apart or to make a hard and fast rule of life or to compile a manual of mortifications or heroic resolutions; we shall not be asked to cultivate our souls like rare hothouse flowers; we shall not, most of us, even be allowed to do that.

What we shall be asked to give is our flesh and blood, our daily life—our thoughts, our service to one another, our affections and loves, our words, our intellect, our waking, our working, and sleeping, our ordinary human joys and sorrows—to God.

To surrender all that we are, as we are, to the Spirit of Love in order that our lives may bear Christ into the world—that is what we shall be asked.

Our Lady has made this possible. Her *fiat* was for herself and for us, but if we want God's will to be completed in us as it is in her, we must echo her *fiat*.

~Caryll Houselander, *The Reed of God*

The Port of the Shipwrecked

Yes, Virgin Mother of God,
you are the intercessor of sinners,
the help of the helpless,
the secure port of the shipwrecked,
the solace of the world,
the mother of the orphans,
the redeemer of the captives,
the joy of the sick,
the comfort of the afflicted,
the salvation of all.

~St. Ephrem of Syria

To Mary We Entrust the Cause of Life

O Mary,
bright dawn of the new world,
Mother of the living,
to you do we entrust the cause of life
Look down, O Mother,
upon the vast numbers
of babies not allowed to be born,
of the poor whose lives are made difficult,
of men and women
who are victims of brutal violence,
of the elderly and the sick killed
by indifference or out of misguided mercy.

Grant that all who believe in your Son
may proclaim the Gospel of life
with honesty and love
to the people of our time.

~Blessed John Paul II, Encyclical Letter,
Evangelium Vitae

Pietà

How sore your grief, Mary,
as you hold the cold and lifeless body of your son
(once warm with beating heart in your own womb)
all bloodied now by death,
and cradle in your arms for one last time
him whom you so often held upon your breast.

Sharing in his pain and passion,
you looked on in agony
as the hands that clung as infant's around your neck
and those feet that pattered long ago about the cozy
home in Nazareth
were cruelly wrenched and nailed fast.

I wonder:

Had you spoken in quiet hours together
of the prophecies and their mysteries?
Had you—with motherly intuition—
read your son's heart and the shadow that
hung over him?

In your nights of pondering,
did you gather strength for this inevitable day?

And now, with a mother's knowing heart,
can you perceive that this stiffening form
upon your lap
(a piece of torn humanity that tabernacles
divinity within)
will soon breathe again
and brim and pulse with life,
all gloriously transfigured?

Looking through the darkness there at Golgotha,
do you already see in your mind's eye
the new dawn promised in three days' time
and tremble to feel again your child's glad embrace?

O wait no longer, Mary,
to entrust him to the grave!
Surrender your son now to Joseph's tomb,
that he might rest awhile from the battle bravely fought
and then descend to death's domain
to claim from Satan there
the victory so hard won for us.

~Jeanne Kun

Mary Teaches Us to Live in the Spirit

The Virgin Mary teaches us what it means to live in the Holy Spirit and what it means to accept the news of God in our life. She conceived Jesus by the work of the Holy Spirit, and every Christian, each one of us, is called to accept the Word of God, to accept Jesus inside of us and then to bring him to everyone. Mary invoked the Holy Spirit with the apostles in the upper room: we, too, every time that we come together in prayer, are sustained by the spiritual presence of the Mother of Jesus, in order to receive the gift of the Spirit and to have the strength to witness to Jesus risen. . . . May Mary help you to be attentive to what the Lord asks of you, and to live and walk forever with the Holy Spirit!

~Pope Francis, Regina Caeli, April 28, 2013

Let Me Dwell with You

O Mother of Jesus,
and my Mother,
let me dwell with you,
cling to you,
and love you with ever-increasing love.
I promise the honour,
love, and trust of a child.
Give me a mother's protection,
for I need your watchful care.
You know better than any other
the thoughts and desires of the Sacred Heart.
Keep constantly before my mind the same thoughts,
the same desires,
that my heart may be filled with zeal
for the interests of the Sacred Heart of your divine Son.
Instill in me a love of all that is noble,
that I may no longer be easily turned to selfishness.

Help me, dearest Mother,
to acquire the virtues that God wants of me:
to forget myself always,
to work solely for him, without fear of sacrifice.

I shall always rely on your help
to be what Jesus wants me to be.
I am his; I am yours, my good Mother!
Give me each day your holy and maternal blessing
until my last evening on earth,
when your immaculate heart will present me
to the heart of Jesus in heaven,
there to love and bless you
and your divine Son for all eternity.

~Blessed John Henry Newman

The Courage to Say Yes to God's Will

Mary answered the angel, "I am the servant of the Lord. Let it be done to me as you say." . . . She said yes to God's great will, a will apparently too great for a human being; Mary said yes to this divine will; she placed herself within this will, placed her whole life with a great yes within God's will, and thus opened the world's door to God.

Adam and Eve, with their no to God's will, had closed this door. "Let God's will be done": Mary invites us too to say this yes, which sometimes seems so difficult. We are tempted to prefer our own will, but she tells us: "Be brave; you too say, 'Your will be done,' because this will is good." It might at first seem an unbearable burden, a yoke impossible to bear; but in reality, God's will is not a burden; God's will gives us wings to fly high, and thus we too can dare, with Mary, to open the door of our lives to God, the doors of this world, by saying yes to his will, aware that this will is the true good and leads us to true happiness. Let us pray to Mary, Comfort of the Afflicted, our mother, the Mother of the Church, to give us the courage to say this yes and also to give us this joy of being with God and to lead us to his Son, to true life. Amen!

~Pope Benedict XVI,
Homily, December 18, 2005

At the Cross: Peace in Place of Struggle

Standing "upright" by the cross, Mary's head was close to her son's bowed head. Their eyes met. When he said, "Woman, behold, your son!" (John 19:26), Jesus was looking at her and therefore did not need to call her by name to distinguish her from the other women. Who could penetrate the mystery of that look between mother and son at such a time? A tremendous painful joy passed between them, and their joy sprung from the fact that they were no longer resisting pain; they no longer had any defenses against suffering; they let themselves freely be immersed in it. Peace had taken the place of struggle. They had become one with the suffering and the sin of the whole world—Jesus, directly, as "the expiation . . . for the sins of the whole world" (1 John 2:2) and Mary, indirectly, through her spiritual and bodily union with her Son.

The last thing Jesus did on the cross before entering the dark moment of his agony and death was to adore the Father's will. Mary was with him in this too. She too adored the Father's will before a dreadful solitude and darkness came over her heart just as there was darkness outside over all the land (cf. Matthew 27:45).

And that solitude and adoration remained fixed there, at the center of her life, until her death when the hour of resurrection came for her too.

~Raniero Cantalamessa, OFM Cap,
The Fire of Christ's Love

The Whole Life of Mary

Keep always represented before your mind, as in a picture, the whole life of Mary, in whom the perfect image of chastity and of virtue shone as in a mirror. Humble of heart, grave in her language, prudent in her designs, she spoke little, respected everyone, and shunned vanity. Her gestures, her walk, the tone of her voice, her whole exterior was in harmony with the supereminent sanctity of her soul. Her walk, her words impressed all who saw or heard her with such profound respect that they seemed not so much to see the body move as her virtues to shine forth.

~St. Ambrose

Imitating Mary's Great Trust

Mary entrusted her life to God's plan for her, and she never took back that unqualified *fiat*, that yes she had given to God. Obviously, she was gifted beyond all of us, but we can learn, little by little, day by day, how to imitate the great trust of Mary.

Our Lady's formula for trust and peace will always remain the same. It is found in her last recorded words in the Gospel: "Do whatever he [my son] tells you!" (John 2:5). Let us pray to her to fill us with great confidence, so that we will never forget that Jesus is always with us. Then we will have nothing to fear.

~Andrew Apostoli, CFR,
Following Mary to Jesus

Mary Represents Humanity and the Church

What does Our Lady represent . . . in this culmination of her journey of faith and commitment to the will of God? She represents humanity, the Church. Having completely followed God's plan to this point, having fully welcomed it, having reached a detachment through faith (to which Abraham was also called), she receives, as a gift, the fullness of the Church. Precisely because she has placed her whole being in God's hands and has abandoned to him all that is most precious to her—her own Son—she receives from God what God has that is most precious—the body of that Son who will live in the Church that is born in the passion, death, and resurrection of Jesus. Mary is the one—more than any other person—who has understood the significance of Jesus' sacrificial offering, of his love for humanity, and of the complete dedication to God's plan that this offering entails. She is now the one who can receive the new humanity as a gift.

This is where our love for the Mother of the Lord should take root. If we lose sight of Mary's journey, we will not be able to understand how God has concretely saved us, giving us to Mary in Jesus since the Church had its beginning in her.

~Cardinal Carlo Martini, SJ,
The Gospel Way of Mary

From "The Virgin Mary to Christ on the Cross"

You messenger that did impart
His first descent into my womb,
Come help me now to cleave my heart,
That there I may my Son entomb.

You angels all. that present were,
To show his birth with harmony,
Why are you not now ready here,
To make a mourning symphony?

The cause I know you wail alone,
And shed your tears in secrecy,
Lest I should be moved to moan,
By force of heavy company.

But wail, my soul, your comfort dies,
My woeful womb, lament your fruit;
My heart give tears unto mine eyes,
Let sorrow string my heavy lute.

~Robert Southwell, SJ

From "The Passion of Mary"

O Lady Mary, thy bright crown
Is no mere crown of majesty;
For with the reflex of his own
Resplendent thorns Christ circled thee.

The red rose of this Passion-tide
Doth take a deeper hue from thee,
In the five wounds of Jesus dyed,
And in thy bleeding thoughts, Mary!

~Francis Thompson

A Woman Clothed with the Sun

A great portent appeared in heaven: a woman clothed with the sun, with the moon under her feet, and on her head a crown of twelve stars. She was pregnant and was crying out in birth pangs, in the agony of giving birth. Then another portent appeared in heaven: a great red dragon, with seven heads and ten horns, and seven diadems on his heads. His tail swept down a third of the stars of heaven and threw them to the earth. Then the dragon stood before the woman who was about to bear a child, so that he might devour her child as soon as it was born. And she gave birth to a son, a male child, who is to rule all the nations with a rod of iron. But her child was snatched away and taken to God and to his throne.

~Revelation 12:1-5
(New Revised Standard Version)

Mary's Assumption

Love carried off that beautiful soul and left in its stead cold and pallid death. O death, what do you do in that sacred body? Do you think you can hold it? Remember that the Son of that virgin has vanquished you and made you his slave. You shall not long enjoy your victory; the love that has placed her soul in that habitation will soon drive you thence. That body, which in life contracted no stain, shall experience none in death. That ark, like the one of old, is made of incorruptible wood.

~St. Francis de Sales

Prayer to Our Mother of Perpetual Help

Mother of Perpetual Help,
you have been blessed and favored by God.
You became not only the Mother of the Redeemer,
but Mother of the redeemed as well.
We come to you today as your loving children.
Watch over us and take care of us.
As you held the child Jesus in your loving arms,
so take us in your arms.
Be a mother ready at every moment to help us.
For God who is mighty has done great things for you,
and God's mercy is from age to age
   on those who love God.
Intercede for us, dear Mother,
in obtaining pardon for our sins,
love for Jesus,
final perseverance,
and the grace always to call upon you,
Mother of Perpetual Help.
Amen.

~Traditional

She Went in Haste

Mary in the mystery of her annunciation and visitation is the very model of the way you should live, because first she received Jesus in her life, then she went in haste to give her to her cousin Elizabeth; what she had received, she had to give. You must be like her, giving in haste the word you have received in meditation.

~Blessed Teresa of Calcutta

90

Mary, Teach Us to Pray Your Rosary

Mary, Mother of Christ, teach us to pray your Rosary as it should be prayed. For these ordinary beads strung on threads hold within themselves all the mysteries of our holy faith and all the main ways of prayer. Mary, Queen of the Rosary, open to us its holy secrets. Let it be our door to the heart of your son, his Father, and the Holy Spirit.

~Catherine de Hueck Doherty

You Can Be a Mother of Christ

Christ's mother is the whole Church, because she herself assuredly gives birth to his members, that is, his faithful ones. And his mother is every faithful soul doing the will of his Father with most fruitful charity toward them of whom it labors until he himself be formed in them. Mary, therefore, doing the will of God, after the flesh is only the mother of Christ, but after the Spirit, she is both his sister and mother.

~St. Augustine

We Delight in Dwelling on Beauty

How beautiful she must have been in soul and body, and how exquisite a joy it is to think of that beauty! For there is a peculiar delight in dwelling on beauty, even if it be only that of a glorious sunset. But there is no beauty like that of a beautiful soul. When, in our intercourse with others, we come across little gleams of grace, we are filled with a sense of beauty which causes us the most exquisite delight. Yet, for the most part, these are hidden among many weaknesses and imperfections. But with our Lady, it was all grace: not a weakness or imperfection was there, so that it is a perfect joy and rest to the soul only to think of her and to draw into our hearts the sense of her spiritual beauty, as we may do each time we say our Rosary.

May our Lady, out of the fullness that is in her, obtain for each of us to comprehend more and more of the "length and breadth, and depth and height" of this great gift of grace, that we may be filled with the "fullness of Christ"! [cf. Ephesians 3: 18-19].

~Mother Francis Raphael, OSD

O Mother of Mercy

O Mother of God and my hope, I am, alas, one of those stray sheep whom the eternal Word came down from heaven to earth to seek, and who now entreats you to bring him back to the fold of your divine Son. The price of my ransom has been paid, and it only remains to apply the merits thereof to my soul. O Mother of Mercy, do not refuse your compassion to a soul for which Jesus shed his blood.

~St. Alphonsus Liguori

Will You See How You Are Loved?

Our good Lord . . . brought to my mind where Our Lady stood in the time of his passion, and said, "Will you see her?" And in this sweet word it was as if he had said, "I know well that you would see my blessed Mother, for after myself, she is the highest joy that I might show you, . . . she is most desired to be seen of my blessed creatures."

And for the high, marvelous, singular love that he has to this sweet maiden, his blessed Mother, our Lady St. Mary, he showed her highly rejoicing, . . . as if he said, "Will you see how I love her, that you might joy with me in the love that I have in her and she in me?"

And also (to give more understanding of this sweet word), our Lord spoke to all mankind that shall be saved, as it were all to one person, as if he said, "Will you see in her how you are loved? For your love I made her so high, so noble, and so worthy. This pleases me, and so I desire that it pleases you."

~Blessed Julian of Norwich

The Treasures of Mary's Consolations

I am the Mother of Mercy, full of sweet love; I am the ladder of sinners, the hope of forgiveness for the guilty, the strength of the afflicted, and the special delight of the saints. Come to me, all you who love me, and you will be satisfied from the treasure of my consolations, for I am good and merciful to all who call upon me.

~Thomas à Kempis, *The Imitation of Mary*

From the "Stabat Mater" (Mother Standing)

Holy Mother, fount of love,
touch my spirit from above;
make my heart with yours accord;
make me feel as you have felt;
make my soul to grow and melt
with the love of Christ my Lord.

Holy Mother, pierce me through;
in my heart each wound renew
of my Savior crucified.
Let me share with you his pain,
who for all my sins was slain,
who for me in torments died. . . .

Christ, when you shall call me hence,
be your mother my defense,
be your cross my victory.
While my body here decays,
may my soul your goodness praise,
safe in paradise with thee.

~Traditional

A Vision of Mary Praying for Humanity

Suddenly my soul was lifted up, and I saw the Blessed Virgin in glory, and when I understood that a woman was placed in such majesty and glory and dignity as she was, I was marvelously delighted; for to see her was joy unutterable. For the Blessed Virgin Mary stood praying for the human race, and I saw her in such shapeliness and power of humanity that I cannot express it. And at this I was ineffably delighted. And while I was thus gazing on her, suddenly there appeared Jesus Christ, sitting by her side in his glorified humanity.

~Blessed Angela of Foligno

From "St. Casimir's Hymn"

Daily, daily sing to Mary,
sing, my soul, her praises due;
All her feasts, her actions worship
with the heart's devotion true.
Lost in wondering contemplation,
be her majesty confessed;
Call her Mother, call her Virgin,
happy Mother, Virgin blest.

She is mighty to deliver;
call her, trust her lovingly;
When the tempest rages 'round thee,
she will calm the troubled sea.
Gifts of heaven she has given,
noble lady! To our race;
She the queen, who decks her subjects
with the light of God's own grace.

~St. Casimir

She Will Come to Meet Your Soul

That loving mother whom you have so much honored during life will come to meet your soul and, with
inexpressible sweetness, will say to you: "You have so
often saluted me as your queen and your mother that
I wish, in my turn, to acknowledge you as my subject
and my child.

"You called me 'star of the sea'; I wish to be such to
you by leading you into the harbor of salvation. You
have said to me, 'The Lord is with thee.' He will be also
with you, for from this moment, you will nevermore
leave me. Behold the hour in reference to which you have
so many times begged my prayers. I have, indeed, prayed
for you, and my Son, out of regard to my prayers, now
opens to you the gates of a happy eternity."

~Paul Le Jeune, SJ

From the Gaelic Litany to Our Lady

O great Mary.
O greatest of women.
O queen of angels.
O mistress of the heavens.
O blessed and most blessed.
O mother of the heavenly and earthly Church.
O honor of the sky.
O sign of tranquillity.
O gate of heaven.
O golden casket.
O couch of love and mercy.
O temple of divinity.
O mother of orphans.
O solace of the wretched.
O star of the sea.
O handmaid of the Lord.
O mother of Christ.
O resort of the Lord.
O graceful like the dove.
O serene like the moon.
O resplendent like the sun.

O cancelling Eve's disgrace.

O regeneration of life.

O enclosed garden.

O closely locked fountain.

O mother of God.

O chaste virgin.

O temple of the living God.

O royal throne of the eternal King.

O sanctuary of the Holy Ghost.

O cedar of Mount Lebanon.

O cypress of Mount Zion.

O crimson rose of the land of Jacob.

O blooming like the palm tree.

O fruitful like the olive tree.

O glorious Son-Bearer.

O light of Nazareth.

O glory of Jerusalem.

~Traditional, eighth century

BIBLIOGRAPHY

Apostoli, Andrew, CFR. *Following Mary to Jesus*. Frederick, MD: The Word Among Us Press, 2008.

Arnold (Brother). *The Book of the Visions and Instructions of Blessed Angela of Foligno: As Taken Down from Her Own Lips*. Translated by a Secular Priest. London: Thomas Richardson and Son, 1871.

Beckx, P., *Month of Mary*. Translated from the German by Mrs. Edward Hazeland. New York: Burns and Oates, 1884.

Cantalamessa, Raniero, OFM Cap. *The Fire of Christ's Love: Meditations on the Cross*. Frederick, MD: The Word Among Us Press, 2013.

Daughters of Charity of St. Vincent de Paul. *St. Vincent's Manual* (Containing a Selection of Prayers and Devotional Exercises Originally Prepared for the Use of the Sisters of Charities in the US). Baltimore: John Murray, 1859.

Drane, Augusta Theodosia. *A Memoir of Mother Francis Raphael, OSD*. Edited by Fr. Bertrand Wilberforce. London/New York: Longmans, Green, 1895.

Hopkins, Gerard Manley, SJ. *Poems of Gerard Manley Hopkins*. Edited by Robert Bridges. Oxford University Press, 1918.

Houselander, Caryll. *The Reed of God*. Notre Dame, IN: Christian Classics, an imprint of Ave Maria Press, 2006. Used with permission of the publisher.

Julian of Norwich. *Revelations of Divine Love*. London: Methuen, 1911.

Kilmer, Joyce, ed. *Dreams and Images: An Anthology of Catholic Poets*. New York: Boni and Liveright, 1917.

M. Therese (Sister), ed. *I Sing of a Maiden: A Mary Book of Verse*. New York: Macmillan, 1947.

Marie of the Incarnation. *The Autobiography of Venerable Marie of the Incarnation: Mystic and Missionary.* Translated by John J. Sullivan, SJ. Chicago: Loyola University Press, 1964.

Martini, Carlo Maria, SJ. *The Gospel Way of Mary: A Journey of Trust and Surrender.* Frederick, MD: The Word Among Us Press, 2011.

Montague, George, SM. *Mary's Life in the Spirit.* Frederick, MD: The Word Among Us Press, 2011.

de Montfort, Louis-Marie Grignion. *A Treatise on the True Devotion to the Blessed Virgin.* Translated by Frederick Faber. New York: Benziger, 1892.

Newman, John Henry. *The New Eve.* Westminster, MD: Newman Press, 1952.

Partridge, F.J.M.A. *The Life of St. Bridget of Sweden.* London: Burns and Oats, 1888.

Philippe (Most Honorable Brother, Superior-General of the Brothers of the Christian Schools). *Meditations on the Most Blessed Virgin.* Translated from the French. Baltimore: Kelly, Piet & Company, 1874.

Rohner, B., OSB. *Veneration of the Blessed Virgin.* Adapted by Richard Brennan. New York: Benziger, 1898.

Russell, Matthew, SJ. *Behold Your Mother! The Blessed Virgin's Goodness and Greatness.* New York: Benziger Brothers, 1909.

Southwell, R., SJ. *The Complete Works of R. Southwell: With Life and Death.* London & NY: Burns and Oates, 1923.

Steele, Francesca Maria. *The Life and Visions of St. Hildegard.* New York: Herder and Heath, 1915.

Thérèse of Lisieux. *Soeur Thérèsè of Lisieux, the Little Flower of Jesus.* New York: P. J. Kenedy, 1912.

Thompson, Francis. *The Works of Francis Thompson: Poems, Vol. 1.* New York: Charles Scribner's Sons, 1913.

Welborn, Amy. *Mary and the Christian Life.* Frederick, MD: The Word Among Us Press, 2008.

Zollner, Fr. John Evangelist. *The New May Devotion.* Translated from German by Augustine Wirth, OSB. Elizabethtown, NJ: Augustine Wirth, 1882.

the WORD among us®
The *Spirit* of Catholic Living

This book was published by The Word Among Us. Since 1981, The Word Among Us has been answering the call of the Second Vatican Council to help Catholic laypeople encounter Christ in the Scriptures.

The name of our company comes from the prologue to the Gospel of John and reflects the vision and purpose of all of our publications: to be an instrument of the Spirit, whose desire is to manifest Jesus' presence in and to the children of God. In this way, we hope to contribute to the Church's ongoing mission of proclaiming the gospel to the world so that all people would know the love and mercy of our Lord and grow ever more deeply in love with him.

Our monthly devotional magazine, *The Word Among Us*, features meditations on the daily and Sunday Mass readings, and currently reaches more than one million Catholics in North America and another half million Catholics in one hundred countries around the world. Our book division, The Word Among Us Press, publishes numerous books, Bible studies, and pamphlets that help Catholics grow in their faith.

To learn more about who we are and what we publish, log on to our website at www.wau.org. There you will find a variety of Catholic resources that will help you grow in your faith.

Embrace His Word, Listen to God . . .

www.wau.org